In Love Abiding

Christine Chapman trained as a social worker and spent twelve years in fostering and adoption work, becoming increasingly aware of the profound effects of unresolved loss on people's lives. She moved to working in bereavement care for the Chester Diocesan Board for Social Responsibility, before becoming diocesan Director of Counselling. She also works as bereavement counsellor at a local prison. Married to a schoolteacher, she is a lay reader at All Saints, Cheadle Hulme and has four grown-up children.

IN LOVE ABIDING

*Responding to the Dying
and Bereaved*

—

CHRISTINE CHAPMAN

A Crossroad Book

The Crossroad Publishing Company
New York

1996
The Crossroad Publishing Company
370 Lexington Avenue, New York, NY 10017

First published in London by Triangle SPCK, 1995
Photoset by Rowland Phototypesetting Limited
Printed in Great Britain

Library of Congress Cataloging-in-Publication Data

Chapman, Christine M.
In love abiding: responding to the dying and bereaved /
Christine Chapman
p.   cm.
ISBN 0-8245-1633-8 (pbk.)
1. Death—Religious aspects—Christianity.
2. Bereavement—Religious aspects—Christianity.
3. Death—Psychological aspects.   4. Consolation.
I. Title.
BV4905.2C435   1996   259'.6dc20   96-20509 CIP

CONTENTS

FOREWORD

The book is intended to help those who approach the bereaved in sensitive and appropriate ways, but with quiet confidence. Written from a sound counselling approach it has a simple theological base which lays the emphasis on the Christian faith of the supporter, rather than on the assumed faith of the bereaved, although significantly it enables the encounter to be within the ethos of the gospel. It has the strength of giving concrete examples.

Each short chapter ends with a helpful original prayer, open to adaptation, written to be relevant to each of the sub-topics which cover all aspects of the responses to bereavement. The book will be of enormous help for lay people who are exercising a bereavement ministry in follow-up care, but professionals, like priests and ministers, will benefit too from being reminded of priorities in approach to pastoral care.

It is not a book on counselling as such, but one which takes the criteria of good practice and applies them to bereavement situations. It is easy to read and has a lightness of touch, and even moments of humour, but more importantly its insights can be readily applied.

+Frank Lambeth

PREFACE

I began writing this book outside my tent in the Swiss Alps whilst waiting – and waiting – for my husband and son to come back from their climbing expeditions. They always have come back, eventually, stooping beneath the weight of rucksacks, ropes and ice-axes, exhausted and exuberant; but they gave me plenty of time to think and write.

Even as I rejoiced with them I was always aware of those whose loved ones do not come back; and those who are bereaved in any way, by accidents, illness, or any other cause. Who do they turn to? Who understands their very individual needs? What is the church doing about these people?

Back home in the Diocese of Chester I have had the privilege of training groups of Christians in caring for the bereaved. Those who attend the courses seem moved by compassion to want to do something for the bereaved in their own churches and neighbourhoods, but most of them feel also a little unsure of themselves, of what they could do, and unsure of their faith should they be asked awkward questions.

I have found that this very lack of confidence is actually an asset at the start. Most bereaved people are not seeking an expert on the subject, if indeed they are any; they are much more likely to want someone to whom they can relate with trust, and who will relate to them in their situation with warmth; who will try to understand how they are feeling, and listen to whatever they feel like saying at the time.

Sister Frances Domenica, of Helen House, Oxford, suggests that we will help most 'by staying alongside as long as we are welcome, by listening, by touching, by gently sharing, by not being afraid to say "I don't know" when that is the only honest answer.'

My aim is to give readers the confidence to meet each different bereavement situation in an appropriate, practical and effective way. I have outlined some theory of the process of bereavement, and some basic rules, but emphasise throughout the unique nature of each bereavement.

I have tried to keep the balance between human bereavement grief and faith in eternal life, beginning with faith the size of a mustard seed, and looking at ways of making it grow.

In the follow-up meetings with those who have

participated in training courses, I have seen that the bereavement care offered by pastoral visitors and neighbours has been greatly appreciated by the bereaved, and often very rewarding for the carers. I myself find the work fulfilling despite its sadness. Perhaps it is in the reaching out in love, and entering into the suffering world of another that we become especially aware of the presence of Christ. I pray that the knowledge of his presence may be with you in your concern and care of the bereaved.

ACKNOWLEDGEMENTS

My thanks to Peter, my husband, for his help in presenting the manuscript for this book, and to all my children for their support and encouragement, especially Alison and Jenny for their constructive criticisms and patient teaching of how to use the word processor. My thanks also to John Weir, friend and critic of my writing, and Lynn, my friend with whom I discussed so much of the material in this book.

1

HOW CAN WE HELP THE BEREAVED?

High on a Swiss mountainside, looking upward to the shining snow peaks, and downward to the wooded valleys, stands a small white church. Its graveyard is ablaze with scarlet geraniums, yellow marigolds, purple and pink petunias – tokens of the vivid memories of the dead still held by those who knew and loved them. One corner is set aside to mark the lives of babies and very young children, whose lives had merely touched this earth.

At the head of each grave is the same simple cross bearing the crucified Christ who had also died, who died for them; at the foot is a covered candle which burns through the darkness of the night, symbolising the Light of the risen Christ who gathers the dead to himself and offers eternal life.

At the centre of the graveyard stands a huge wooden cross, bringing together past, present and future, proclaiming the God who loves, who suffers, who cares passionately both for those who have died and those who are living.

1

As we look upon those who plant the flowers, clinging to their vivid memories, seeing no further than the cross of suffering on the grave of their loved one, some of us will ask: how can we reach out to them, comfort them, enable them to see also the Light of those burning candles, the hope of the eternal life which is here for them on earth as well as for those in heaven?

There is no quick or easy way. As their love and their lives were so closely entwined with the lives that have passed on, so the pain of their separation is deep and lasting. It may be a long time before any light is glimpsed. But even so, their pain need not be locked in to their grieving hearts. There is relief in opening up, letting some of that grief burst out and be received by others; there is comfort in sharing, being listened to by those who would give themselves in love and compassion.

There is a flicker of light through the ministry of listening, which may be learned and practised by those who care. There is no need to try to think of the 'right' thing to say or do – there is no right thing – but there is a need to reach out with the love of Christ, to hear, to stay alongside, to break through the isolation of personal grief, to bring back into the body of Christ.

Very slowly, with the help of those who will listen, and love, and accept, the acute pain of loss

may be eased; very slowly, with the companion-
ship of those who will support, encourage, and
accept, the strength and will to go on living may
be found, until the bereaved can glimpse for themselves a flicker of light in the darkness, a small
surge of joy in a relationship, or thing of beauty, a
feeling that life can be meaningful for them again
in a different kind of way, even without the one
who has died.

Their dead will never be forgotten; the flowers
will be tended and replanted with just as much
love. But memories may become more bearable,
happy as well as sad, with thankfulness for the
good times that were shared. Some may realise
that they have somehow become stronger, that
their priorities have changed; they appreciate love
and beauty more, they have more to offer, perhaps even a deeper faith. Then they may see that
the light, which had seemed to go out, had all the
time been burning on their behalf; that God had
been there all the time, conveyed in part through
the caring of friends.

If you are one of those ordinary, caring
Christians who wants to reach out and help the
bereaved, but feels unsure; if you are humble and
poor in spirit, yet sensitive and able to listen, then
these words are for you. No one ever really knows
how another feels, but you can listen and find out;

you can be alongside, you can love and support.
You will not be alone. The Christ who died is
risen and with us always. He will be with you, and
with the bereaved, and it does not matter what
you hope to achieve, only what he will achieve
through you.

Eternal Father of us all,
who sent your Son, Jesus Christ,
to live and suffer and die
that we might know eternal life with you;
grant to us an awareness of his empowering love,
that we might reach out to those who are bereaved,
and bring something of your love and grace to them.
We ask this is in the name of Christ,
Lord of the living and the dead. Amen.

2

WHAT OF OURSELVES?

It is in our weaknesses and humanity that we will be most fully alongside others in their hurt, wounded condition. It is our real selves, just as we are, and not as we think we ought to be, that is the most valuable thing we can offer. And so the first step in setting out to support others is to look at ourselves and our own attitudes – with courage and honesty.

How do you actually feel about dying? Have you been able to face your real feelings when you have lost what is most precious to you, or when you have been bereaved? What is the present state of your faith?

I do not think you can expect to be completely sorted out in these matters, or to have the answers, whatever they may be. But I should like to ask you to try to face your real human feelings – of fear, panic, hurt, resentment, guilt – honestly, with acceptance, and never, never feel ashamed of them. For when we are at our weakest, then we may be most open to Christ.

It is a simple fact that when we face those feelings we would prefer not to have, a block is removed, they lose their power over us and become more bearable and can be accepted as part of our true selves. It may help to talk them over with a friend we can trust. Further, if we cry to Jesus in our pain, and tell him about our fears and doubts, the way is cleared for him to be with us where we are, and for us to receive his peace and comfort, his strength and healing. Our relationship with him is open and wholehearted. He never rejects those who are open to him. He came to heal the sick, not the righteous, and who among us is not sick in some respects?

Another reason for facing our real feelings courageously is that they have a way of surfacing when in contact with similar feelings in those we have gone out to help. Suddenly we find that repressed guilt or pain threatens to take us over. We identify and say, 'I know, that happened to me when. . .' and before we realise it we have burdened the suffering bereaved with our own problems. There may be a place for identification, mentioning that we too have experienced a similar loss. But that is all. It is our very real responsibility to deal with our own feelings first, and if any unexpected uncomfortable thoughts are triggered off, then we must put them aside firmly, and look at them afterwards.

So before going any further, try asking yourself these questions. It may help if you write out your answers. And pray that God will give you the grace to consider them honestly, and to accept your thoughts. They are probably much the same as other people's!

☐ Do you think seriously about your own death, that it might happen tomorrow, or even today? Or do you push it to the back of your mind, to think about another time?

☐ Are you afraid of dying, or afraid of the unknown?

☐ Are you afraid of being totally dependent on others?

☐ What do you think you ought to do in preparation for your death?

☐ Are you willing to hand over your body, mind and spirit to Jesus? Do you trust him?

☐ Have you thought positively about life after death? Can you look forward to it?

☐ Think of an unborn baby, safe in his mother's womb. Might not he, if he were aware, be very worried about going through an uncomfortable birth to an unknown life outside? Who is waiting for him at the moment of birth? Who will be waiting for you at the moment of death?

Now read how Jesus faced his own imminent death in Luke 22.39–45, and then read his words of reassurance in John 14.1–4.

Jesus was afraid of his death, so full of anguish that his sweat was like drops of blood falling to the ground. The answer to his prayer came not in the removal of the cup of suffering, but in strengthening to bear it. He prays for us now, and he will pray for us at the hour of our death, that we will be with him, where he is now. He went ahead to prepare just the right place for each one of us. He understands any fears that we might have.

Lord Jesus Christ, give me the grace to face my
*   own death with courage, and faith.*
Help me to prepare myself, to deal with past
*   wrongs, and relationships.*
Let me allow your Spirit to enter the dark parts of
*   my life and personality;*
Thank you for the eternal life I have through
*   knowing you, Jesus Christ, my Lord and*
*   Saviour. Amen.*

3

LISTENING TO
THE DYING

We have asked ourselves questions about our own attitude to dying, and death. It is quite possible that you may be asked to see someone who is terminally ill, or that you are wondering whether or not to see a neighbour who may be dying. I feel sure that there is a place for those outside the immediate family to visit, for it is often easier to talk more openly to those who are not closely related. I should like to introduce you to someone I met at a local hospital who knew that she had only a short time to live. I will call her Margaret. She gave me the privilege of sharing her thoughts about living, and dying. . .

Margaret sat on the bed, thinking. She wanted to tell the family herself that the operation had not been a success and she was going home because there was nothing else the hospital could do for her. She felt a bit rejected, and a bit frightened too, but she knew it was no good giving way to these feelings. She had always been the strong one in the family, the one who kept everyone else going. Well, she would stay the strong one, in spirit, anyway. She had coped before when things were bad, and now she just hoped she would cope with this.

'All right, Mrs Stanley?' The doctor was passing her bed with a couple of students, and the sister.

'Yes, thank you, doctor,' she replied automatically, and the doctor moved on. He looked relieved.

'Hey, wait a minute, doctor,' Margaret called after him. 'I'm *not* all right, am I? I want to know what to tell my husband; I want to know about painkillers; there's a lot I want to ask you.'

It occurred to Margaret that almost for the first time in her life she had the upper hand over someone as important as a doctor. He stopped, motioned to the students to go on, and sat down on the bed.

'Well?'

Margaret asked her questions. She felt detached, as if she were talking about someone else. She asked him to speak in words she could understand, whereas he felt much more comfortable using medical terminology and hiding behind his professional image.

'Thank you, doctor. I really appreciate you talking like that, just like an ordinary person. I won't bother you any more. Thanks for all you've done.'

The doctor shook hands awkwardly. He was glad that was over, and very glad that his other patients were either recovering, or not asking difficult questions.

Margaret lay back on the pillows, surprised at herself. She was not afraid of important people any more. She did not need to be afraid of anyone now. She wished she had realised that earlier. From now on she would be a person in her own right, instead of everyone's servant. She would look after her family as long as she could, then she would ask them to look after her. She would have to ask, she knew. From now on she would live as she wanted, and let people know her needs.

'Can I get you some coffee, Margaret?' Her friend in the next bed interrupted her thoughts.

'Yes, please. Two sugars, and plenty of milk.'

Yes, she would cope. She was not afraid of people any more, but she had to admit she was frightened about the unknown. She wondered if there was anything else she had missed out in her life. Perhaps she could find some nice, ordinary person to talk to about God. Somehow, she had never had much time for God in her busy life. . .

*   *   *

How would you be if Margaret were a friend or neighbour of yours, and you went to see her? You are not sure how much she knows about her medical condition or how she is feeling, and you are anxious in case you say the wrong thing. You could act as if everything was all right and she would get well again; or you could go when you knew someone else was there and there would not be an opportunity for a heart-to-heart discussion; or you could try to convey to her that you want to be the best friend or neighbour that you can be to her, in the way that she would like you to be. How do you do this?

Remember – no one ever knows exactly how anyone else is feeling. Margaret was a coper, but you cannot assume that she is coping with this. Her family have always seemed very close, but she may, or may not, want to show her real feelings to them. She may welcome the opportunity to talk to someone outside the family.

So do look really pleased to see her as you go in; as indeed you are, however worried you may be at what you should say. Express that affection for her in some way. Perhaps the visit could go something like this:

'Hello, Margaret, it *is* good to see you. What a lot of cards and flowers you've got.'

'Yes. I didn't know I had so many friends.'

'Do you mind if I sit down for a minute; or have you had a lot of visitors today?'

'Bring that chair up, do. It would be nice to talk for a bit.'

Now ask her how she is in a way that gives her the opportunity to answer in her own way. Speak quietly and gently, looking at her with the concern you feel:

'So how are things with you now?' Wait for her answer. It is tempting for us to fill in the pauses, especially if we are nervous. But it is these very pauses which give the other person space to think what she wants to say. If she replies, 'All right, thanks', then that has to be all right for us. We are not there to probe. But it may be that she tests you out as to how honest she can be with you, how much you can take.

'Well, not so good, actually.'

'I'm sorry.' Try to allow another pause. There is nothing much you can say except, perhaps, a tentative 'How do you mean?'

'They've sent me home because there's nothing more they can do for me. The operation didn't work.'

'That sounds as if it must have been an awful shock for you?'

'Yes. I was shocked. I feel quite rejected. Actually, I feel quite frightened. . .'

And away she goes. You have shown her that you do want to know how she is, that you want to understand how it feels for her, that you respect her and are willing to try to come alongside her however painful that may be. Listening like this can be healing for Margaret, leading her toward the wholeness that God wants for her.

She might even ask you about God. You may feel you would like to run for the expert. But remember that she has asked you, and not the vicar. You do not need to know everything. Just tell her simply what you believe. It could be something like this: that you do believe in God who loves and cares deeply about Margaret; that he expressed his love by sending Jesus Christ to earth, to live as a human being, and to suffer in all the ways people suffer, and more, because he took upon himself all the sin and wickedness of this world; that he died in the prime of his life; that God, in his divine power, then raised Jesus from death to a new kind of life in a new resurrection body, appearing to his disciples for a short time to explain what it all meant.

It means, to Margaret, that God is a God of suffering love, suffering for us, suffering alongside us. It means that Jesus revealed to us the resurrection to new life which can be ours as we turn to him and know him. It means that Jesus is there for us in heaven, and there for us on earth, through the Holy Spirit. He will give us his strength and comfort as we talk to him, and his peace even in our own suffering. He will give us his life – eternal life – on earth and in heaven.

That is the hope that could be Margaret's. She may know it already, or she may ask you either for reassurance or because she wants to know. If she asks you, tell her in the only way you can. Jesus will use your words to bring his truth to Margaret as she faces her death.

Lord Jesus Christ,
we pray for those who are dying,
those who may not want to die just yet,
those who are afraid, or unprepared.
Grant to us the gifts of your wisdom, and courage.
Give us the words we need
that we may be true neighbours to the dying;
And grant to them the peace that only you can
give, as they go forward to be with you. Amen.

4

FAITH: IS OUR
FAITH ENOUGH?

How can we increase our trust in Jesus – our trust that he identifies with us in our fears; that he can give us the strength and courage we need; that he will take our lives and deaths in his hands; that he will give us eternal life? What is the state of our faith now?

Let us begin with that tiny grain of faith, the size of a mustard seed, that we know when we are at our more confident, and look at one of the best known sayings of Jesus: 'For God so loved the world that he gave his one and only Son, that whoever believes in him shall not perish but have eternal life' (John 3.16).

Jesus is not saying we have to reach a certain stage of goodness before we can receive eternal life; he is not saying that we must be more disciplined and cut out our more dubious ways; or that we must work out and understand the Christian religion with our minds. He is just saying that we must believe in him.

Well, we do believe in him, even though our belief may only be the size of a mustard seed. And most of us have had this sort of belief far longer than the criminal who was dying on the cross next to Jesus. Yet Jesus said to him: 'Today you will be with me in paradise.'

Take a few minutes or more to read these words of Jesus in Luke 23.40–3. The man had probably never given Jesus a thought before that day. And all he did now was to rebuke the other criminal for mocking Jesus, admit that they were both being punished justly for what they had done, and turn to Jesus and ask, 'Jesus, remember me when you come into your kingdom.' That was all. Not a lifetime of strong practising faith, and certainly not a life of doing good works, but rather, faith, the size of a mustard seed. Yet he was to be with Jesus in paradise as soon as he died.

We can find that very comforting in our moments of doubt as to the amount of faith needed for eternal life. And it is surely a comfort to be passed on to those who are troubled about the apparent lack of faith in their loved ones who have died.

Who knows what goes on in the mind of those approaching their death, even in the last seconds of their lives? Any Christian nurse will tell you of the regrets so often expressed by the dying; or their hesitant questions about God. And to those who have never known the real Jesus we may recall the credal statement that Jesus Christ descended to the dead before he rose again in order to make himself known to those who had never known him.

Yes, there are some who reject Christ right to the end. That is their decision. But there are many who finally turn to him in their hour of direst need, and their loved ones may know nothing about it.

Let us never underestimate either our own wavering faith, or anyone else's. Maybe our loved one never went to church, maybe he did reject the gospel for most of his life. But who are we to judge whether or not he entered the kingdom of God after his death? All we can do is to entrust him to the infinite love and mercy of Jesus Christ who came to earth not to condemn, but to save.

*　　*　　*

And now – meet Elsie, who was in the same ward as Margaret. She needed to be accepted just as she was, and she did have a grain of faith, though you might not have thought it when you first met her.

Elsie was sad that she was nearly at the end of her life. Sad to be leaving behind so many friends. Just as she was getting the hang of it all. Her first husband had left her – just walked out leaving her with a couple of kids. Still, she had managed, somehow. Her convent upbringing had given her some structure to her life, and she had always felt that Someone, somewhere, was giving her a hand.

Then there was Bill. She had always had a soft spot for Bill even though he was a bit violent after a drink or two. But he never deserved prison. He was never the same after that. And he had never taken to the next two kids who had come along when he was inside. That had been tough, trying to stop them all going the same way. But Someone, somewhere, had kept her going.

And now, after all this time, a grandma several times over, she had found a man who loved her, and wanted to look after her. Jim. Okay, so he was the lodger and ten years younger, but that was all right. He had promised to look after her now as long as he could because, he said, she had taught him how to love. And that, decided Elsie, is what it is all about. Someone, somewhere, told her that, and she would stick to it.

She ended our conversation by saying 'Do you know that priest who always hangs around when he's not wanted? Well he's wanted now. . .'

I would have loved to be a fly on the wall as she made her confession to the priest. In her way, Elsie was prepared to meet her Maker, to put a name to that Someone, somewhere, who had somehow got her through this life.

Father, we thank you that you sent your Son,
  Jesus Christ,
to bring all who believe in him to eternal life.
We thank you that Jesus accepts us with love,
however small our faith in him.
We come to you now with the faith that we have,
and ask you to build on it,
and help us to grow in faith and love
of Jesus Christ, our Lord and Saviour. Amen.

5

FAITH: IN ETERNAL LIFE HERE AND NOW

Of course Elsie, or the penitent criminal, or anyone else who turns to Jesus only at the end of life, misses out on the whole new dimension of life that Jesus Christ gives us here and now. For eternal life is not something that begins after our death; it begins the moment we turn to Jesus, and ask that we might know him, and know God through him. Jesus said, 'Now this is eternal life: that they may know you, the only true God, and Jesus Christ, whom you have sent' (John 17.3).

Eternal life is the new life that the risen Christ gives us as we acknowledge the futility of our lives without him, acknowledge our powerlessness to be good by his standards, acknowledge the human sins and weaknesses that we all have; and turn to him, just as we are.

We tend to be reluctant to do this when life is going well for us. But if we stop for a moment and ask for the grace to see ourselves as we are, as God sees us, then the reality of our human condition will be clear. We are probably as good – and as bad – as the next person, but are we the person we would like to be, realising our full potential, growing in wisdom and love, living the way God intends us to live, becoming the person God created us to be? Are there not always things in our lives, or our relationships, or situations, that hold us back from being our true selves, that make us resentful and unforgiving, inhibited, or afraid? Can we look back on our lives so far and think, 'I am perfectly happy with myself, and feel I can face judgement (however we think of judgement) with a clear conscience'?

Jesus, in his humanity, is surely the only person who could answer these questions positively. His only desire was to be the person his Father wanted him to be, to do his will on earth, to be able to say at the end of his life, 'It is finished. I have lived and died as my Father willed me. Into your hands, Father, I commend my spirit.'

If we are to be completely honest with ourselves, most of us would feel that we have a need of a Saviour who would free us from all that holds us back, nourish and sustain us in the present and lead us forward in the way that is God's will for us.

But some of us fear that Christ will not accept us as we are. We feel unlovable, or just not worth bothering about. Maybe no one else has ever taken the trouble to make us feel we have any worth in ourselves, so why should God?

God is not like that. Jesus wanted us to think of him as we would think of an ideal, loving father figure who loves us whatever we are like; the father who suffers with us for what happened to us in the past, who longs to free us from others' dominating influence over us. And as for our worth in God's eyes: Jesus said, 'Look at the birds of the air. . . Are you not much more valuable than they?' His concern, remember, was for the poor in spirit, who knew their need of God.

So we may be sure that Christ accepts us now, and at the hour of our death, with outstretched arms. It is what he has always wanted for us. It is what he was prepared to die for – that in him we might be right with God, and right with our-selves. But he does far more than just accept us. For, once we look to him in our weakness and realise that he is seeing us with eyes of love, then the Holy Spirit, the Spirit of Christ, begins to feed that little seed of faith. It starts to grow – sometimes quickly, sometimes slowly – to pro-duce in us the strengths and gifts of the Spirit, freely given as we need to build up ourselves, and others, in the body of Christ.

It does take time and prayer, Bible reading and fellowship with other Christians, to continue growing in faith and wisdom and love. And there will be times when we slip backwards and have to begin again. There are always beginnings but never an end; we may know the beginnings of eternal life now, just where we are in our lives on earth. At some stage in our growth we will pass through death and know the fullness of eternal life where our questions will be answered, our love will be made perfect and we shall become what we truly are, in Jesus' glorious presence for ever.

Lord Jesus Christ, we thank you that you accept us just as we are,
with your tender love and understanding.
Give us the courage to accept ourselves, to face our pain and fears and sins,
and to confess them to you freely.
Give us the grace to be open to your peace and healing,
and to know your will for our lives.
So may we be freed to help others as we ourselves have been helped,
and to trust in you in our living and our dying.
Amen.

6

FAITH: IN LIFE
AFTER DEATH

Should we continue to pray for those who have passed on into the fullness of eternal life? For those we continue to love though they are no longer with us? Both the church and the Bible teach us very firmly that it is wrong for us to try to contact the dead for they have moved to a realm which is far beyond our human comprehension. Jesus just asks us to trust in him about life after death.

I remember being put on the spot about praying for the dead by a little five-year-old girl whose teenage brother had tragically taken his own life. 'Do I still say, "God bless Mike" when I say "God bless Mummy and Daddy" in my prayers?' she asked. I replied 'Yes', with complete conviction. She could not pray for his salvation – that is in Jesus' hands – but I do believe she could entrust him to Jesus and pray for him with all her love. In this way she would let him go into the compassionate hands of God and still express her love for him.

St John wrote his revelations of life after death. He saw 'a great multitude that no-one could count, from every nation, tribe, people and language, standing before the throne and in front of the Lamb. They were wearing white robes and were holding palm branches in their hands.' And he was told, 'These are they who have come out of the great tribulation; they have washed their robes and made them white in the blood of the Lamb. . . For the Lamb at the centre of the throne will be their shepherd; he will lead them to springs of living water. And God will wipe away every tear from their eyes' (Revelation 7.9, 14, 17).

It is in this context that we pray for our loved ones – safe in the joyful company of those who have allowed themselves to be purified by Christ, tenderly cared for by the ascended Christ who is healing them from all pain and sorrows and leading them gently into the fullness of eternal life.

It may comfort some to take a look at the experiences of those who have been very close to death, or those who have 'clinically died', and through the effects of modern medical techniques, have been resuscitated back to life. Obviously, these experiences cannot be accepted as 'gospel truth', yet I have been impressed by the sincerity of people I trust, and I accept their recollections as true to them.

A former vicar of my church once spoke of his

illness as a ten-year-old boy, when he had nearly died of pneumonia. He said it was as if he became outside of his body, looking down on himself in bed. And he felt so enfolded in 'a glory of love and light' that he was reluctant to be drawn back into his body. Afterwards his parents told him they thought he had died. 'One thing I know for certain now,' he said, 'I shall never be afraid of dying.'

To be contrasted sharply with these experiences are the attempts of those who have gone to mediums in order to contact the spirits of the dead. These mediums often have a psychic knowledge of people's lives and thoughts; they will tell the bereaved things about themselves and about those who have died. They will offer a sort of reassurance – that their loved ones are alive in the 'spirit world', and looked after by the spirits of those who have died before them. Spiritualists do not mediate through Jesus Christ, for they do not believe he is the Son of God or Saviour of the world. They encourage members to expand their earthly consciousness to greater awareness of the spirit world by tuning in to the spirits there.

But where are these spirits? Who are they? If we seek reassurance in ways excluding Christ, then we will be led to a whole realm which excludes Christ and we will lose sight of our Lord and Saviour. If we needed to know more, then Jesus would have told us. He told us as much as we could understand. St Paul puts it this way: 'Now we see but a poor reflection; then we shall see face to face. Now I know in part; then I shall know fully, even as I am fully known' (1 Corinthians 13.12).

We may know eternal life in this world through our relationship with Jesus; we may glimpse the beauty and radiance of the kingdom of God in moments when we are granted an awareness of the presence of God. But for the rest, let us read again those comforting words of Jesus to his disciples on the subject of death:

> Do not let your hearts be troubled. Trust in God; trust also in me. In my Father's house are many rooms; if it were not so, I would have told you. I am going there to prepare a place for you. And if I go and prepare a place for you, I will come back and take you to be with me that you also may be where I am (John 14.1–3).

*We thank you, Father, that our loved ones who
    have died are safe in your keeping.
Help us to let them go to you in perfect trust,
because you love them, and us, with infinite love.
As you have prepared a place for them, prepare us
    also,
that where they are, and you are, we too may be,
through Jesus Christ, our Lord and mediator.
Amen.*

7

THE BALANCE BETWEEN CHRISTIAN FAITH AND HUMAN GRIEF

Not long ago I received a newsletter from a Christian organisation which contained a paragraph about a young man who had been a popular leader at a summer camp my family had attended: 'It is with much joy that we announce David's promotion to glory by our Lord. We invite you to rejoice with us at a service. . .'

It took me a few minutes to realise that this young man who had been so loved by so many children had actually died. He had been in the prime of his life, with a lovely young wife and two small children, and was an effective evangelist who brought many young people to know and love Jesus Christ as their Lord and Saviour.

I felt angry with the writer of that newsletter, angry that he or she seemed to feel that David's death was a matter for joy first and foremost, angry that God was seen to be authorising a promotion, like a reward for good service.

And I felt concern for his wife and children.

Were his church, or the Christians with whom he worked, trying to understand their feelings of grief? Were they supporting them in their loss? What were his wife's feelings of loneliness, help-lessness, yearning, anger? Was she surrounded by the love and understanding of friends who would be there for her as she grieved and tried to live a meaningful life again? I could only hope so.

Some time later, when I had coped with my own feelings of anger and grief, I found I could begin to rejoice for David himself. Yes, he would be with his beloved Lord now; yes, he would have joined the glorious company of the redeemed, worshipping God in his glory along with the saints in heaven. I could be glad for David now.

I could see also the balance which Christians particularly need to achieve in bereavement. Their faith in eternal life *is* a matter for rejoicing, on behalf of the one who has died. But if the relation-ship has meant anything to them, then they must grieve for themselves; for the loss of all that the relationship meant, for the life that has been cut off, for the loss of that person. There is nothing wrong with personal grief. Jesus wept when he heard of the death of Lazarus. It can seem to be a belittling of our past relationship if Christians tell us we should be rejoicing.

God does not take away the pain. Grief, it is

said, is the price we pay for love – and I think most of us would want to have loved. Only when the weight of grief is beginning to lift a little will we be aware of the presence who has been with us all the time, loving, suffering with us. Until then, God sends other people to bring his love in a tangible way.

*   *   *

So how does the newly bereaved person feel? What are the symptoms of grief? We know that each experience of bereavement is unique, because each person, and each relationship is unique. Yet there is a general pattern of grieving which it is useful to recognise, and helpful to the bereaved if you can reassure them that they are perfectly normal to be feeling these things. When a death first occurs it may be for those who are close as if the world suddenly stops. There is no going on and no going back – just the dread of the present moment, too much to take in all at once. The more sudden and traumatic the death, the deeper the shock. Even the most natural, expected death brings some shock. Things have changed, and will never be the same again.

Stay with the bereaved person, if you can. They are not themselves, and if they need to make decisions they need the stabilising influence of one they can trust.

Perhaps they cannot, and will not grasp the reality of what has happened. 'It must be a mistake; it's someone else; you've got it wrong.'

This is normal for a little while, but if it continues for a few days, try to persuade them to see the body, if appropriate, and see that someone goes with them.

There may be an inability to feel appropriate emotions. People often switch on to 'automatic pilot' and appear perfectly in control as they prepare for the day of the funeral. Do not assume that they are coping well with the death. They are probably living in a sense of unreality where feelings are numbed. It may last until the funeral is over.

Then, the acute pain of missing the deceased has usually set in. No one can do what the bereaved want above all – that is, to bring back the one they have lost, to restore life to normal. But never underestimate the support you can be by just being there as long as they want you. The comfort, support and practical help of friends who will just listen and be there with their love and acceptance is invaluable. Since the bereaved may find it impossible to know the love of God at this stage, they can at least be aware of yours. Perhaps you could think of it as helping to bring something of God's love to them in a tangible way.

Grief may manifest itself in physical ways, such as dizziness, nausea, headaches, stomach upsets, palpitations, insomnia and exhaustion. These can be frightening, especially if the deceased suffered from the same symptoms, and a visit to the doctor can be helpful and reassuring.

Occasionally you may be aware of 'repeat prescriptions' for sedatives over a long period of time. This is rare now, but if it is happening try to encourage a discussion with a doctor. In the long run drugs only delay the grief process.

Nearly all bereaved people want, and need, to talk about the one they have lost, for that person is still part of their lives and must not be dismissed or forgotten as if he or she never existed. Reminiscing is part of the healing process, part of seeing the person as they were, warts and all, part of trying to understand and make some sense of it all. They may find people are embarrassed, do not want to hear, or think they are being morbid. Even the family may get fed up with the same stories over and over again. The outsider can do better, offering a fresh, interested ear, knowing how necessary it is if the bereaved are to begin to come to terms with the death. Reminiscing usually cheers up the bereaved, and it is useful to encourage it towards the end of a visit, in order not to leave them in a state of distress or depression.

Depression comes and goes all through the grief process. It is discouraging for the friend, and you may have to accept that there are days when the bereaved just cannot be bothered to be welcoming. That is all right. Try again in a while.

Depression tends to occur when the bereaved one is totally exhausted from bearing all the overwhelming emotions. It can be seen as a period of dull rest which they need. Towards the end of such a period, you may be able to encourage a little creative activity like gardening, sewing, or something they used to do and enjoy. Creativeness does lift depression but it has to be at the right time.

Before looking at the more violent emotions that are a normal part of the bereavement process, I should like to express concern for you, the friend and supporter. You may feel very helpless in the face of others' depression, and may well absorb their sense of despair and hopelessness. If this happens, do not wait until it has sunk in to your very depths, but offer it to Christ as soon as you are on your own. Offer it with confidence.

*Lord Jesus Christ, I come to you now, weary and
heavy-laden with the sorrow and despair of my
friend.
I commit her now into your loving care, and I
commit myself to you for rest and refreshment.
Give me your peace now, and give me hope in the
new life which only you can bring,
my living Lord and Saviour. Amen.*

8

THE JOURNEY ON
THROUGH BEREAVEMENT

The three strong emotional states which nearly all bereaved people – but not everyone – feel are anger, guilt and anxiety. This is well known, but the intensity of these emotions may overwhelm the bereaved, and leave onlookers quite helpless. Nevertheless, they are a normal part of the grief process and need to be experienced, and expressed. 'Why did this happen to her? She never hurt anyone. It's all so unfair. Why did God let it happen? Where is he in all this?' The bereaved are not expecting answers to their tortured questions. They are merely expressing their anger and confusion. Anger which is expressed tends to die down after a while. Anger which is suppressed may turn into bitterness, resentment, and then depression. It is hard to take for the one who is there to listen, but helpful if you can absorb it. But do make a point of handing it to Jesus on the cross, and receiving his peace. You are not alone.

Guilt is nearly always felt by the bereaved simply because neither they nor the deceased are perfect, and no relationship is ever perfect. There will always be things they feel they should or should not have said or done. Try to listen to outpourings of guilty feelings without contradiction, but with warm acceptance of the person. Probably they have been guilty; so have we all. Ask if they feel that the deceased would forgive them in the light of the relationship as a whole. They may like to write a letter of explanation, and penitence, or they may be encouraged to go to their priest or minister to express their guilt before God, and receive forgiveness. Normal guilt will usually subside into regret after a time; regret can be tolerated.

The bereaved may suffer from great anxiety, according to how dependent they have been on the deceased. Such anxiety is understandable for there has been a change in identity – they are no longer a husband or wife, but a widow or widower; they no longer share the parenting but are now a single parent – or not a parent any more. A friend who has been a life-enhancer leaves a big gap in the life of the survivor. There may just be a general loss of confidence, a fear of being alone, a fear of not being able to cope. Try to help the bereaved identify the loss, and what it involves for them; it helps to reduce the general confusion, and to become clear-headed. Be with them in that loss with acceptance and love; when they are ready, gently encourage their efforts at building up a new life, becoming the new person that they have to be now.

Loss of faith is a common part of the bereavement process. It may be that the bereaved has to think out a personal faith from the beginning again. It is easy to think God is on our side when all is well with us. It can be very difficult to find God in the midst of overwhelming grief. It may be hard to go again to the church they always attended together, or where the funeral service was held. Offer to go with them for a while if you can. And hang on to your own faith, even if you do not have the answers to their questions. Do not be afraid to say, 'I don't know.' God is there even though they cannot know him just now. Be patient, and pray. Many of the bereaved do eventually come to know God in a way that they had never known him before.

Faith in eternal life must never ignore the reality of pain and suffering in the human life that has been bereft of a loved one. True, if the journey through grief is to lead to healing, it must be viewed in the light of eternity where life and death properly belong. But it must also be acknowledged in human, finite terms, expressed to, and heard by those who bring reassurance, warmth and love. So many people say that the only thing

that kept them going was the support of friends
who let them talk, who let them express their
anger and desolation, and who still stayed with
them.

> Lord Jesus, we pray that we may be especially
>   aware of your presence as we go to be with those
>   who are bereaved.
> We place the time we spend with them in your
>   hands;
> help us to be the loving, accepting person they need
>   us to be.
> Give us the wisdom to know when to be quiet.
> Be with us, and with them, at this time. Amen.

9

THE TIME IT TAKES –
AND ACCEPTANCE

It may be a long, long time before the weight of this human grief begins to lift, even a little. Some talk about a sense of reassurance they are given. The mother of a young man, who had been killed by an avalanche when climbing, tells how she was in her bedroom one evening, thinking of him and wishing that he had continued to go to church when he had left home. After a time the room seemed to fill slowly with light which engulfed her whole being, and she 'knew' that he was very much alive in a different kind of way, completely happy, completely at peace. The light faded, but the peace came to rest within her, and after that she began to feel that she could be glad for him, and that her grief was for herself. Not everyone is given this kind of reassurance, and there seems to be no reason why some people receive these experiences and others do not.

We who want so much to bring the comfort of the Christian faith can feel very helpless as we stay alongside those who seem to be only oppressed by their grief, and unaware of the presence of God. It may be that the bereaved have to think out a personal faith right from the beginning. The faith they had has been shaken to its very roots. Their God seems to have abandoned them and left them comfortless.

Try to be patient with them, with yourself, and with God. Pray that his love may reach them through you, or through anyone or anything else. Think of the trees in winter which look so lifeless, black and stark against the cold grey skies; yet, as you look closer, you will see that the buds of new leaves are surely there, at the tips of each branch, waiting for the breath of spring to bring them to new life. Even the birds are silent – yet their song may sometimes be heard in the early dawn, and at the dusk.

And there will be moments when the bereaved notice that the sun is shining, when they realise they can laugh again, when they appreciate the friendship of those who go on giving of themselves without the reward of receiving anything back. Only moments, for the darkness descends upon them again; but the moments come more often, and for longer at a time.

There will always be those, particularly the old, who have had so many years with the one they have lost, who never want to live on their own, who cannot recognise that the spring of new life is there for them also. These are the ones who need several friends who are prepared to go on visiting, and bringing their own life to comfort and support. But the majority of the bereaved do respond to the spark of God's Spirit within them. This spark will never die. It will be fanned to a small flame by the love of others. In time it will bring the bereaved to a state of acceptance when they can think and talk about the one who has died with a lessening of pain, or a level of pain which is tolerable. The deceased is never forgotten, but can be rememebered with pleasure.

Acceptance comes as the bereaved gradually learns to 'let go', and feels motivated to build up his own life again, to find joy and meaning in living again. He may actually need permission to let go, permission to enjoy himself again, and you can encourage this when the signs are there. God does intend healing for the broken-hearted, and fullness of life again to the bereaved, but it will be a new and different kind of life from the one they knew before.

Lord Jesus,
help us to be patient as we see the slow progress of
    bereavement grief.
Help us to be mindful of the creation process of life,
    and death, and new life again.
Help us to offer, and to go on offering, the kind of
    support that encourages the growth of new life
    on earth.
Help us to draw our life and love from you, that
    we might give out what we receive.
Jesus, our Living Lord. Amen.

10

CHILDREN GRIEVE TOO

If you go to see a family who are grieving, do remember to notice the children in that family. There is a common tendency to single out the adults, and overlook the feelings of the children – or even persuade ourselves that they are not suffering.

Children do grieve too, but not in the same way as adults. Young children have not learned to articulate their feelings and they have not the words to communicate them. Children under about five or six have difficulty in seeing death as permanent and may ask continually, and pain-fully, when the one who has died is coming back. They tend to respond to the death they do not understand with anxiety, fearing that their needs will not be met, and expressing their confusion indirectly by complaining of stomach-aches and pains, not wanting to go to school or playgroup, or by sudden changes in behaviour. Like the mother of a five-year-old who was late meeting her from school one day, and found a very angry little girl who shouted at her for not coming when the other mothers came.

'I'm sorry about this,' she said to the teacher. 'She seemed to change overnight from such a happy little girl to this aggressive child who won't let me out of her sight, and is so demanding. I can't seem to do anything right in her eyes.'

Her teacher looked surprised. 'I think she's coping very well really. She must miss her little brother dreadfully. Rachel, do you think you could take this book for me to the office?'

As Rachel left the room, her mother explained to her teacher just how it was at home. 'No, I don't believe she misses Jamie at all. Even just after he'd died all she said was, "Can I go out to play now?" You'd think she'd have more feelings for him than that.'

'Oh, but she does miss him,' said her teacher. 'She goes to his grave nearly every day and looks as if she's talking to him. Maybe I shouldn't have let her but I can see her from the classroom and she always lets me know she is going.' The school was a small church school, separated from the church by the graveyard.

'Only last week she asked if the whole class could go and sing "Happy Birthday" to Jamie. He would have been two, wouldn't he?'

'Yes. Well, I am surprised. She never told us. She won't ever talk about him at home.'

Rachel came back into the classroom but

refused to hold her mother's hand. She looked sulky and cross. Her mother blinked back her tears and made a huge effort. 'Rachel, shall we go and buy some flowers and put them on Jamie's grave? You can choose them.'

The little girl's whole face lit up. 'Can I come too, really? He likes yellow flowers. He loves buttercups. Let's pick them now. Oh, Jamie, you'll be so happy.' And for the first time since Jamie had died, his mother felt something like a warm glow within her. She had never thought of them visiting the grave together.

Perhaps we adults try to protect our children from suffering. It is very distressing for us when we cannot solve their problem, or even make it better. So we tend to exclude them from activities round the funeral, or convince ourselves that children do not suffer, or are resilient, and get over things quickly.

Children *do* grieve for someone they have lost, who has been part of their lives. If they are jollied along, distracted, or sent away, the chances are that they will never feel 'right' about that death. They may even develop a pattern of suppressing their emotions generally, or they may feel haunted by a sense of sadness and confusion every time they are faced with the death of someone they have known. But if they are allowed and encouraged to grieve in their own way, and in their own time, they are likely to be well-prepared and able to cope with situations of loss and death for the rest of their lives.

While very young children tend to express their grief indirectly, children over the age of about six are beginning to grasp the finality of death and may attempt to express their feelings – if they are given encouragement to do so, and if they are allowed to share in the family grief. But even if they are seen to be grieving openly, a few minutes later they may be out playing with friends as if their tears had meant nothing. It is not that they are callous, or heartless. I think that children and young people have a kind of defence mechanism which will not let them grieve for long at a time for they would not be able to stand it. And their returning to familiar play is their way of adapting, and giving themselves time to accept what is new and very disturbing.

11

CHILDREN'S GRIEF –
SOME HELPFUL HINTS

I should now like to suggest a few ideas which have helped other children, and may help the children you know.

Most children over the age of about five do need and do want to talk about the one who has died, and may go over and over the death until they have it right in their own minds. We adults need to listen, and give time to them, to find out how each child sees the death and what are her particular feelings about it.

Some children, however, seem unable to do this. They may sense that it is too painful for parents; that it is not okay to mention the deceased's name. They may feel that somehow it is their fault that the death has occurred. Young children do not always distinguish between feelings and actions; they tend to think that someone must be to blame. Suppose their disobedience or anger against a parent caused him to die? They have to keep quiet about that.

Most children of between about three and eight years old express their feelings through play. So do give them time and space to play, and try to be with them at times, responding, but not leading. Dolls, or figures that represent members of a family, may say or do surprising things in the words of their player:

'Woody is looking everywhere for his daddy. He's very, very cross with him because he's gone away and left him. Very cross. Very angry.'

And he beats Woody's head against the wall making a loud noise.

'Is that how you feel? Very angry with Daddy?'

'I don't know. Sometimes. He shouldn't have gone. He shouldn't be happy with Jesus. He should be happy with me.'

A few words to explain again why Daddy died, and how sad this makes everyone feel, is likely to set it right in the child's mind. Try to make it clear that Daddy did not choose to die and leave them all. It was the illness/accident/sickness of mind that caused it.

Drawing can be another way of children getting out what they do not know how to put into words. Finger-paints or big crayons can make very satisfying splodges or shapes, often in black at first. I have found little point in asking a child under five what a splodge means. It just seems to express the blackness inside her. But it is better out on paper than mouldering around inside. When other colours begin to creep in you will know the child is beginning to feel better about everything.

Older children may like to make up a scrapbook or photo album with pictures of themself with the one who has died. This will encourage them to talk about the deceased; to remember him as he was and to keep those memories alive. An adult can be very helpful sharing in this activity.

If at all possible, try to encourage some sort of routine about mealtimes and bedtimes, and be consistent about discipline. It is difficult when everything has changed, but it does provide some sense of security, and reassurance that their needs will still be met, and that life for them will still go on amidst the grieving. Otherwise, children have their ways of demanding the security they need in less than welcome terms.

Most of all, grieving children need to be listened to. The difficulty here is that they will talk when they want to, not when adults ask questions, and it is a matter of catching them at the right time. This, of course, tends to be just at that point when parents have said goodnight and are preparing to leave, glad to have a bit of time on their own. It is hard for parents, who are hurting so much themselves, to give from the emptiness inside them, to give more love and patience than they feel they have. All I can offer here is that it does become a bit more possible as the parent becomes stronger and more of a whole person instead of half a person if they are widowed. The family has changed. Although it will never be complete again, the ones left have to try to become a working whole, and right from the beginning it helps to include all family members in what is going on.

This brings us to the all-important question of the funeral. Should children be allowed or encouraged to attend, or is it better that they go to school as usual, or join the family afterwards? I suggest that we shall only know what is best for a particular child if we ask her. Most children seem to know whether or not they want to go to the funeral and it seems to work to take them at their word. As a general rule, children do like a sense of things being done properly, with due ceremony and ritual. It gives a sense of completeness, of decency, of openness. If parents are too upset to be aware of the child's needs at the funeral, then it is best for another adult member of the family, or a close friend, or a teacher, to take charge and explain what is going on.

Children do need explanations, not just at the time of the funeral, but right from the beginning. They need the whole procedure of dying explained clearly to them: the cause of death, the sad feelings the family are left with, what happens to the body, and the life that continues in a different way after death. If these questions are not dealt with, the child is likely to ask people outside the family – and may receive some strange answers:

'Grandad has become a star in the sky.'

'God has taken Mummy to be with him in heaven.'

'John is happy now, at rest with Jesus.'

Do not tell children beautiful lies which they will have to unlearn later. Do not make God out to be a baddy who takes away loved ones. And do not feel that you must always have an answer. It is all right to say, 'I've wondered about that too. What do you think?'

It does seem that children can accept the most painful information, so long as it is given in a loving, secure environment. Tragic accidents, illness, suicide, even murders need to be told to them by close relatives or friends, though it is not necessary to go into every detail. Otherwise they will hear from some other source, and will never feel they can ask those nearest to them. They may imagine what could have happened, and fantasies are usually worse than reality. So explain that hospitals and doctors can usually cure sickness, but occasionally there is no cure. Explain that it is extremely unlikely that the child themself will die soon, nor will the surviving parent. What happens after death could be explained something like this, in a way that seems reasonably comfortable to the parent: 'When we die we don't need our bodies any more so we leave them behind to be buried or cremated. The Bible suggests that God give us a new body, rather like a plant above the soil which grows from the seed below (1 Corinthians 15.35–8). So when our bodies die we go on living in a different way, with Jesus and all the other people who have died. We don't know much about it except that Jesus called it heaven and asked us to trust him about taking us there. Even now we can ask Jesus to look after our loved ones.'

Children need to understand death in their own terms and within their ability to comprehend. They often have a very down-to-earth and simple attitude to what we adults frequently complicate.

None of us has concrete answers to what happens after physical death. But most children do accept Jesus in their own way. Even if he has no place within the family, he will have been introduced to them at school. Trusting Jesus comes more naturally to a child than to many adults. So rely on the child's trust in Jesus, and give the explanations needed in a loving secure environment, and you may give something more precious than you realise at the time. You may acknowledge, or encourage faith in the Lord who is always with us, who is King of earth and of heaven, who loves and cares for us all, now and eternally.

Lord Jesus Christ,
who told the disciples to let little children come to you;
bless, we pray, those who have lost someone they
love;
lead them to those who will comfort and listen;
give to them a glimpse of heaven that is meaningful to
them,
that they may trust you in the process of life and
death,
and know you as their heavenly friend. Amen.

12
UNDERSTANDING BEREAVED TEENAGERS

It is teenagers who have special difficulties facing bereavement. They are already coping with a different kind of loss as they shed their childhood and struggle to find their new identity as young adults. Their inner resources may be drained; their confidence at its lowest ebb; their outer environment which has provided some stability may be crumbling away before their very eyes. If, at this vulnerable stage in their lives, they lose one who has been a significant part of their lives, they may feel at a total loss as to where to find the comfort, security and normality of life that they need.

Their situation is complex at the very least. If it is a member of the family who has died, they may or may not be included in the family grieving. Some adults take all the grief on to themselves and cannot respond to, or even admit that their children, too, have their grief. If the household is predominantly depressed with grief that excludes the younger members of the family, then a teenager is likely to take himself off to a more normal atmosphere with friends, and return home for meals and a bed, and the disapproval of others; or he may withdraw to his bedroom and create his own refuge playing loud music or indulging in some other activity which is unacceptable to the rest of the household.

If the relationship with the dead parent has been poor, albeit temporarily, then he may feel tremendous guilt. He does not share this with the surviving parent, who cannot in any case support him because of his or her own grief. And his teenage friends do not seem to know how to cope.

Sometimes the teenager is put into the position of being either 'the man' of the family, supporting his mother, or 'the housewife', who is expected to do the household tasks and look after the younger brothers and sisters. He or she will usually comply, but not without some resentment about the imposed loss of freedom. Although the situation probably cannot be changed, teenagers will certainly appreciate some acknowledgement of all they are doing – and surviving parents are notoriously backward at giving this.

If the death is outside the family, parents may just be unable to help in the way the teenager wants; while at school, or work, or in the community he wants to be seen as cool and coping and like everyone else. So he suppresses his feelings and finds himself strangely alienated, anxious, and probably very angry that his parents do not seem to understand and his peers do not want to be involved.

Many teenagers will appear to undergo a change of personality when they are bereaved; some become suddenly passive, withdrawn, dependent and uncommunicative; others become quite aggressive and independent, refusing to let themselves be helped, projecting their negative emotions on to parents or teachers and refusing to let anyone get close.

It is obviously good for teenagers to express their strong feelings appropriately while allowing themselves to be loved and supported. But an aggressive or uncommunicative teenager who insists on playing it cool can be somewhat off-putting to those of us who long to help.

Let us begin by refusing to let ourselves fear rejection, and by being prepared to go to grieving teenagers with our natural love and concern, asking, if it seems appropriate, what it is they want in this situation.

I remember coming alongside – literally, on the pavement – our next-door neighbour's son, Neil, aged fourteen, whose father had died just a week earlier.

'How are you doing, Neil?' I asked, perhaps a little nervously.

'I'm not doing, if you really want to know,' was his angry reply. 'No one talks to me. It's all Mum, Mum, Mum.'

'Well, yes,' I said guiltily, remembering how I had gone in to his mother and not thought even to speak to Neil.

'No one wants to talk to me about Dad,' he said. 'And no one wants to listen to me talk. As a matter of fact that's all I want to do – just talk about Dad. But everyone keeps changing the subject at school, and some of them don't seem to want to know me any more, as if I have a disease.'

I could see that Neil was in danger of becoming a very aggressive young man unless he found people who would let him talk. A word with his form teacher helped in conveying his needs to his classmates.

Another young teenager, Sue – whose friend, Di, had been killed on her bicycle – insisted that her parents just did not understand. They kept telling her it was time she got over it now, and to spend less time in her bedroom and more out playing tennis and swimming as she had used to. What did Sue want? She wanted to meet with those who had been friends of Di's and play the music that Di had liked. Everyone's parents had discouraged them because they thought it was morbid.

I have found that most teenagers do know how

they want to deal with bereavement, but they are not always very good at communicating this, or they assume that adults will not understand. Some find great comfort in writing a diary, often in secret; others may be encouraged to write a letter to the deceased, saying all the things they would like to have said before, even saying they were sorry for the way they behaved.

But it takes patience, and the will to accept the individual teenager's own way of expressing his feelings. Only he will know the right way for him – and that may not be easily understood by adults. I should like to record the reactions of a friend of mine upon visiting her son's grave and finding a group of teenagers 'lolling around smoking and laughing, and messing about with the flowers'.

13

AT THE GRAVESIDE
OF THEIR FRIEND

A group of fourth-formers were sitting or lying by the grave of their friend, Andrew, who had been knocked down by a car outside school and killed. One of them had seen it. No one voiced the unthinkable – that it could have been them instead of, or as well as, Andrew. They almost wished it had been them. Andrew had more guts than the rest of the class put together. 'Remember when he tipped his chair back just too far and crashed over just as the Head walked in?' 'Was it seven or eight pints he downed at that party?'

One of the boys, who just sat there saying nothing but puffing away at a cigarette, got a scrap of paper out of his pocket and wrote something on it. Then he stubbed out his cigarette, wrapped the paper round it, and stuck it on the grave with his penknife. One of the girls began to sob quietly and he put his arm round her. She leant against him, comforted for a while.

'What are you doing here? What are you doing to my son's grave?'

They started guiltily as Andrew's mum

appeared, and watched in horror as she snatched the penknife from the grave, saw the cigarette stub, and read the writing on the paper: 'Andrew, remember the first fag we shared?'

'We're sorry, Mrs Wilson, we didn't mean anything wrong. We were just talking about him.'

Andrew's mother did not seem to hear. 'I didn't know he smoked,' she said.

'Well, he didn't much. We all have one sometimes. He was one of us.'

They started to leave, but she called, 'Don't go, please. I don't think I knew Andrew properly, especially these last few months.' She looked at the girl: 'Are you Kate? You were – his girlfriend, weren't you? I'm sorry I didn't meet you before.'

Kate filled up again. 'I wish he was here. I miss him like anything.'

'Yes. So do I.' There was a silence, not an awkward one, but a sharing silence. Then Andrew's mum said, 'I'm glad you came here. Come whenever you like. In fact I'd like you to come round to our house after school one day and talk some more about the things you did together. He used to talk a lot about his friends.'

'Thanks, Mrs Wilson, we'll do that. See you.' They left her by the grave, feeling a bit uncomfortable – especially about the fag – but quite comforted in a way. They felt oddly appreciated, as if they had shared something important together.

And my friend remarked how, when she had recovered from her initial reaction, she had felt very comforted to see his friends grieving, and looked forward to having them round and learning things about Andrew that she never knew.

'Though I don't suppose I shall know everything,' she said ruefully, 'He *was* a teenager.'

Father, we thank you for our teenagers,
and we think of them with love and sometimes
    sadness,
and sometimes repentance for the times we have not
    tried to understand.
Help us, we pray, to relate to them in a way that
    they can accept,
to respect their way of grieving and to be patient.
Help us to make their grieving smoother as they
    struggle to grow into the adults you intend them
    to be.
Bless our teenagers who have lost someone they
    love. Amen.

14

THE DEATH OF
A CHILD

I hesitate even to touch on the death of a child, as
every bereaved parent says, 'No one can possibly
understand unless they've been through it.' But
we may still find ourselves close to those who
have lost a child and they would not want us to
avoid them. I write, therefore, as one who has
listened to and cared quite desperately about many
parents who have been bereaved and I do think we
can offer something, as long as we do not claim to
understand how they feel.

I will start with the story of Vicky, for I felt I
could offer nothing. Yet there was something
these young parents wanted of me. They wanted
the reassurance from a Christian that what they
were thinking could be right.

Roger and Helen lost their little girl, Vicky,
aged five, and I was asked by their vicar to see
them. I prayed for the grace to be what those poor
parents needed me to be.

They were very young, attractive and tear-
stained. Neither had any church allegiance or any
grasp of the Christian faith. Yet they were both

saying, through grief-stricken tears, 'God has somehow made it all right. He has been there all the time. Life without Vicky is unbearable. But we know she's gone through to live with Jesus.'

How were they so sure? Helen tried to explain it. She said she could see a sort of plan, beginning at the moment of Vicky's birth, when she had known that she would not have this precious baby for long. She had vowed there and then that she would value each day of her life. When Roger announced her birth in the paper he added, '. . . a precious gift from God', though he admitted he did not know why.

Vicky was not a very comfortable sort of child. She asked too many questions: 'How was the very first rabbit born if he didn't have a mummy?' and at Christmas time: 'Why do you buy me so many presents when you say there are some children who don't have enough to eat?'

When she was four they took her into town to hear carols sung round a Christmas tree and to see the nativity scene.

'Is that really baby Jesus?' asked Vicky.

'Well, it's a model of Jesus,' said Roger realistically, and Helen added, 'Jesus died a long time ago.'

'Why is it just a model of Jesus?' asked Vicky in

a disappointed voice. 'I'd rather go and see my baby cousin who's real.'

Later that night Roger read Vicky the Christmas story. She was interested, but critical.

'Why does it say Jesus was the Son of God if Joseph was his daddy?'

Her parents could not answer any of these questions but, like Mary, they pondered them in their hearts and waited.

The following Easter Vicky was playing on the floor while the television happened to be broadcasting an Easter service. Suddenly she jumped up and ran into the kitchen. 'Mummy, Jesus isn't dead. He's alive. Look, the television says so.' Sure enough, across the television screen were the words, 'Jesus Christ is risen. He is alive today!' She then went upstairs and got the book, *Stories of Jesus*, given to her by her godmother, and with her mother's help read it all the way through. Her parents were surprised that it became her favourite book, and she began to talk to Jesus almost as she would talk to her friends.

Just after her fifth birthday she said, 'I don't really think I want to die. Do you want to die?' That evening she began to be ill. The hospital doctors diagnosed a rare virus picked up from the soil. They thought it could be treated. Then began seven weeks during which Roger and Helen lived at the hospital watching the poison spread through Vicky's body. She was in a coma for most of the time, and the doctor told Roger that her brain might be affected. Her body was bloated and her parents felt they had already lost the Vicky they had known.

Then, one morning, Vicky suddenly looked her old self again. Her face had become normal, and her mind was as lucid as ever. But she was suffering pain, for the first time. Helen said she knew then that Vicky was going to die and because of the pain she deliberately 'let her go' and asked God to take her. Almost immediately Vicky fell asleep and seemed to pass from this life into death, looking just like the sleeping little girl they had so often kissed goodnight at home.

When I was asked to see Roger and Helen I felt as inadequate as I have ever felt. For what comfort could there be for parents who had lost an only child through some rare disease? But what they wanted from me was acceptance of the way they saw it all; that the God they had never known before Vicky was born had somehow guided her life, and her death; that the Jesus she knew was caring for her now in the delightful relationship that Vicky seemed to have had with him. And, second, that Helen had been right in 'letting her go' to God; that she had not somehow contributed to her death. For some reason they did not feel they could say these things to relatives and friends and they needed confirmation from a Christian that it could be so.

It did not lessen their personal grief; they had lost their beloved child, and nothing could bring her back. Their comfort was the thought that Vicky was as special to God as she was to them, and now they felt they wanted to get to know this God who had entrusted them with parenting her.

* * *

Parents who have lost a child seem to find most help from the company of others who have also lost children. Some hospitals have their own groups for bereaved parents; there are groups for those who have suffered cot-deaths, those who have had stillbirths or neonatal deaths, and there are the Compassionate Friends, consisting of bereaved parents helping other bereaved parents. Information about these organisations may be found at a local Citizens Advice Bureau.

But these parents still live in their individual neighbourhoods, and still have their places of worship, of work, of various activities – of which you may be a part. Do not add to their feelings of isolation, but be prepared to come as close as they want you to be, and to listen to what they may want to talk about.

One difficulty which seems common among all parents who have lost a child is that husband and wife grieve in different ways and cannot always understand each other. 'It's as if there's an unseen barrier between us now,' said one woman. 'I *think* he's grieving, but he won't talk about it and he doesn't want me to either.'

The strains on a marriage which suffers the death of a child are immense. Some parents – a few – can grieve together. And if one is feeling particularly weak then the other manages to be strong and supportive. But many more experience very different feelings about their loss, and have very different ways of coping. Men are still not expected to show their feelings openly. They may feel they have to be strong and protect the rest of the family – and suddenly crack months or even years later.

If you know a couple who have lost a child, try to encourage them to respect each other's way of coping even if they do not understand it. One bereaved father admitted that the only time he let his grief out was when he was driving his lorry on his own. He never told his wife this, and for a long time she built up feelings of resentment against him for not seeming to care. Try to encourage each to be patient with the other until they can feel more at one with each other again.

Never feel you must know the right thing to say to bereaved parents. You never know what they are going to say to you. Accept where they are and how they are feeling just then. And do not worry about whether they are Christian or not. Just be there for them, as long as they want you there.

Loving Father,
we thank you for the gift of children,
and all that they offer to us;
and we thank you for the privilege of bringing
*   them up for you.*
We know that all little ones are specially precious
*   to Jesus;*
we thank you that you prepare a special place for
*   them in your kindom.*
Comfort all bereaved parents, we pray,
and help them to know your suffering love for your
*   beloved Son*
who died that we may have eternal life through
*   knowing you,*
and from knowing Jesus Christ, our Lord and
*   Saviour. Amen.*

15

THE DEATH OF THOSE WHO HAVE NOT REACHED CHILDHOOD

There are other deaths of children which are not usually talked about openly: death by stillbirth, death by miscarriage, and death by termination of pregnancy. I include these because I have come across so many deeply grieving parents who suffer the additional hurt of living in a society which does not seem to count these as real deaths.

'To be told, "It's all for the best", or "It's a blessing in disguise", or "You can always have another one", is so intensely hurting,' said the mother who had experienced both birth and death at the same time.

'The hospital was wonderful. The staff couldn't have been more understanding. They let us stay with her as long as we liked. They took photographs and gave us other things to remember her by. But when we got home, no one wanted to see that precious photo, or talk of her by her name. They seem to prefer to think that she never existed and that we could not have loved her. Catherine will always be one of our children, and we shall never forget her.'

That mother found it most comforting to talk to others who had suffered stillbirths, who understood. But she would have liked, also, to have been able to share her memories of Catherine with her friends and neighbours.

Those who have had a miscarriage are also likely to be at the receiving end of others' well-meant remarks; 'It's nature's way of dealing with handicaps', 'Better now than later', or, 'You'll be pregnant again in no time.' What anger that brings to the bereaved ones; what isolation. Does no one understand that the life that has begun – and ended – has to be grieved for and can never be replaced by another? The day when the baby would have been born is indeed a sad one for all who have shared in that pregnancy, and it will be appreciated if others acknowledge it with a letter or a visit or flowers. Remember too that the father has his feelings. We tend to think more of the mother's needs and forget the father.

Those who have suffered a miscarriage do not have the comforts and the acknowledgement of a funeral service. But it will be helpful to many if prayers can be said and the little life committed into the hands of God. It is my personal belief that life can never be stopped, but that there is a place in heaven for all whose lives have begun and ended before they experienced the outside world.

That may or may not be a comfort to those who have had their pregnancy terminated by choice. Whatever we may think about abortion, we must remember that the woman who discovers an unwanted pregnancy and who seeks medical advice will be given the option of termination, and may have strong pressures from others to make that decision. At first she may feel relief. But then, sometimes months or even years afterwards, she may feel terrible guilt about what she has done, and the silence, or disapproval, of those who believe in the sanctity of human life will not help her.

She, too, needs to express her grief to one who will listen, and know forgiveness and acceptance by God who is the creator of all life. There will be no prayers said officially for that baby, but it is never too late for us to say our own prayers both for the baby and for the parents.

Having a child is possibly the most basic function in which we ever participate. It is our share in the process of creation. Losing that child who has been an integral part of its parents takes away their wholeness for a time, and leaves them hurting and in need of healing. Let us then take very opportunity to listen to them, to acknowledge their grief, and to pray for them and their babies.

Father of all, creator and giver of life,
we commit to your tender love and mercy
all whose lives ended while still in the womb or at
* birth.*
And we pray for their parents, that their grief may
* be healed,*
and that they may know your love and care for
* them, and for their babies,*
now and eternally. Amen.

16

SUICIDE

There are some deaths from which we shrink and which make us feel more than ever inadequate. But if a relative or friend of your neighbour takes his own life, and if you are there – are you going to bury your head in the sand, or are you willing to offer what support you can, and to learn how they are likely to be feeling? Try to read on. You will be needed, if you are there.

'Why did he do it? Why didn't he talk to us? If only we'd known he was unhappy. Where is he now? Why. . .?'

The questions go on . . . and on . . . and they are never answered. Suicide is one of the most difficult deaths to begin to come to terms with.

Relatives and friends who thought they had known him well are left in a state of shocked horror: 'We'll never forget finding him. . .' And bewildered guilt: 'What did we do wrong?' And confusion: 'He wasn't the person we thought he was.' And rejection: 'Why didn't he tell us?' And anger: 'How could he have done this to us?' The relationship they thought they had is broken – and can never be put right, in human terms. No one knows what to say, how to comfort. The isolation seems unbearable. Their questions can never be answered.

Do not leave them now. The only comfort available to them is the love and support of friends and relatives who will stay with them in their pain and grief. If you feel you cannot bear it, how much worse do they feel? Talk to them about the kind of person he was. Many will be afraid to mention his name, but those closest to him have the same task as anyone else who is bereaved – to talk about him, and his life, and to try to find meaning in it all.

Although nearly all reminiscing will inevitably get round to the unanswerable, 'Yes, but why?' it is essential not to get stuck there. A little boy in Helen House, a hospice for children in Oxford, who knew he was going to die, said, 'God has the answers, we have the questions and only when we come to the end of our life will he tell us the answers.'

So talk about what you do know: the good things about his personality, his generosity perhaps, his kindness and sensitivity, his gifts; those occasions when he had been a delight to have around. Let the bereaved see that his whole life was not wasted.

Sometimes suicide occurs through the mistaken notion that the person does not want to be a burden to others. One woman who had taken her own life left this tragic note to her daughter: 'Now you are free to live your own life, without me to hold you back.' The daughter needed all the support she could get in the guilt and pain with which she was left, but after a while she began to see that she must build up her own life and become her own person in order to find some meaning in it all. In this way her mother's death would not be in vain. It took five years for her to learn to live on her own confidently, to hold down a responsible job, to work out her faith again, and to respect and even love herself so that she was able to love and relate well to others. There seemed to be a sense of redemption in her response, as new life grew out of that terrible death by suicide.

Never suggest a possible meaning for anyone else; that can only come from the bereaved. But by our readiness to go and to listen prayerfully, to be with them in their intense pain, to hear the expressions of guilt and rejection, anger and despair, opportunities will arise to support the bereaved in the way ahead that is right for them. The pain may never be completely healed in this life, but it will become more bearable if it is shared; the anger will subside if it is allowed to be expressed; the guilt will lessen if the bereaved feel accepted and loved by others; and the life that ended so tragically will be seen to have greater worth as the personality, gifts, relationships and events of that life are discussed and explored with someone else.

It must always be wrong for anyone to take the initiative in ending the life that God has given. But is there any sin that is unforgivable? The bereaved may need guidance in their perceived view of the church's attitude to suicide. We remember the time, not so long ago, when the church would not offer a Christian funeral for those who had committed suicide. It is different now. The church – now – says, 'Trust in God about this. Only God in his infinite love and compassion knew what was in that person's mind as she took her own life.' And the funeral is likely to reflect this truth.

But does the church speak loudly enough? As members of the body of Christ, the church on earth, we *must* bring the love of God to those facing the desperate devastation of their lives and faith through the suicide of a loved one. Through this kind of support, over a long time, they may be helped through the unanswerable questions to face their future courageously. And some will be led to a closer relationship with the Lord who knows how it all was, who understands, who loves both the one who has died and the ones who are left, with the deep unconditional love that only he can offer.

It takes a long time, and inexhaustible patience to offer this kind of support. But know that what you offer, in the name of Christ, is actually sharing in the redemptive work of our Saviour himself. You may feel inadequate – as we all are – but you will not be alone, and your offerings will be part of Christ's outflow of love and compassion and healing.

Loving Saviour, you understand us in our
   weaknesses,
and ask only that we put our whole trust in you.
Give us the grace we need to touch the hearts of
   those bereaved by suicide,
that they may know your love and forgiveness,
and continue their lives in the healing that only
   you can bring.
May they know reconciliation with the one who
   has died,
and closeness to you, who died that all may be
   united with the Father of us all, the God of all
   life and death. Amen.

17

FORGIVING THOSE WHO HAVE CAUSED THE DEATH

I should like to mention the issue of forgiveness, for I find that many of those bereaved by accidents, or even murder, for which someone is clearly responsible, cannot begin to come to terms with their situation until they start to try to forgive those who have caused it.

I do not say this lightly, and I am aware that anyone who has suffered such a devastating tragedy could feel very angry at the mere suggestion of forgiveness, but I mention it because I have seen the lack of a forgiving spirit to be such a destructive force in the lives of bereaved people.

Most of us have to confess that forgiveness is not part of our natural make-up. We are much more inclined to demand an 'eye for an eye and a tooth for a tooth' – and a life for a life. It is fair, and we clamour for justice as we see it; especially if the one who has died is the victim of another's careless or drunken driving, especially if he has been killed deliberately as part of a political statement, or murdered. The desire for revenge and the terrible bitterness that overwhelms the bereaved are easily understood by all who know them. Yet these very natural feelings act as a destructive poison to the lives that are left, and can prevent the healing that God longs to bring about to their deeply hurting souls.

In recent years there has been a trend toward expressing forgiveness. It started with Senator Wilson whose daughter was killed in the Enniskillen terrorist bombing. Others ask how they can forgive when there is no penitence. Perhaps forgiveness is a Christian concept alone. Perhaps it is too much to expect. I do not know. But I have come to see that it is an essential part of the ongoing lives of those who are suffering such devastation. Without it they wither, and die to the fullness of life that could still be theirs.

A priest whose little son had been killed by a drunken driver writes, 'I knew I had to write a letter expressing our forgiveness to that man – for our sake as much as his.' As he struggled to write he knew he had to be dependent totally on the grace of God to give him the will to forgive. Yet as he wrote, he began to feel a peace that could only be from God. And he was able to grieve now, sustained by the presence he trusted.

I am not suggesting that we tell those bereaved

in this way that they should forgive. They will probably see no reason why they should. And if there is a court case involved, they will almost certainly not be able to contemplate forgiveness until it is over, which can take a year or more. But do spend some time praying that God will give them a forgiving spirit, and meantime, pick up on any hints that they might consider it.

During my weekly visits to a local women's prison as bereavement counsellor, I am beginning to understand the terrible feeling in so many prisoners' hearts that they can never forgive themselves for what they have done, and that God – whoever he is, wherever he is, but whom they know is there, and whom they fear – cannot forgive them either.

Those imprisoned for manslaughter, or 'lifers' who are there for a major part of their lives for a murder they have committed, have a great deal of time and space in which to think. Many seek the comfort and acceptance of the chaplain's room, or church services. Many can only survive with the help of tranquillisers to numb the guilt they cannot live with and the feeling of being condemned by the loved ones of those they have killed, and by God.

No one ever seems to think of communicating these feelings to the bereaved who are left only with the pain and horror of what has happened, exacerbated by their anger and hatred toward those who have caused it. A member of a self-help group for those whose relatives had been killed by hit-and-run drivers said, 'We don't think in terms of forgiveness for the simple reason that no one has ever come forward to express penitence for what they've done.' Yet penitence, I know, is often there, locked in the mind of the offender.

One 'lifer', whom I have seen many times, assisted her boyfriend in murdering an old woman for her money seven years ago. She tells of her remorse and horror at her part in it. 'The worst time is at night when I see this horrible face filling the room – I think it's the devil; he won't leave me alone.'

Can there be forgiveness for this woman? I think of Paul – St Paul – who was 'breathing murderous threats' to followers of Christ. Remember how he was converted so dramatically to the one he had persecuted; how the disciples had some difficultly in accepting him at first, but then how powerfully he was used in the service of Christ. I think of Jesus himself, as he was nailed to the cross by jeering soldiers, saying, 'Father, forgive them, for they do not know what they are doing.' I wonder if there is any sin that is unforgivable by God, if there is genuine repentence on the part of the sinner.

Another 'lifer', as a teenager, was involved in the murder of a teacher. Now, twelve years later, devoted to the Lord who shows that he still loves her despite what she did, she wants to give her life in his service and hopes one day to be ordained. We may doubt the appropriateness of this – but who better to witness to the forgiveness of God than one who had sunk to the depths of such depravity, and repented?

I am aware that the examples I have given are from a women's prison, and many who cause deaths may feel no such remorse for what they have done. Yet we pray, 'Forgive us our sins as we forgive those who sin against us.' Is there any limit to forgiveness? When Peter asked our Lord how many times he should forgive he thought that seven times was more than enough. But Jesus' reply, 'Not seven times, but seventy-seven times' suggests that there should be no limit.

Isaiah writes of God, 'For my thoughts are not your thoughts, neither are your ways my ways. . . As the heavens are higher than the earth, so are my ways higher than your ways, and my thoughts than your thoughts' (Isaiah 55.8–9). The more we learn of God's ways the more it seems that the greater the sin the more God wants to forgive the sinner. It is not easy to grasp. Real forgiveness on our part is a grace, offered by God to those who ask for it, and are willing to try to receive it. It is not reasonable, or fair, but it does seem to bring a sense of peace and it does seem to clear the way for light and love and healing to flow in. It is surely a grace worth praying for, both for ourselves, and for others.

Father, we pray for those who find it impossible to
   forgive
and think of them with understanding and
   compassion.
We know that they cannot be healed while they
   have such feelings of hatred.
Lord, shine your light into their darkness
that they might begin to know forgiveness for those
   who have hurt them so deeply.
We ask this in the name of Jesus Christ who
   forgave those who were nailing him to the cross.
   Amen.

18

VISITING THE BEREAVED

Most of us, at some time in our lives, are in a position of wondering whether or not we should go to see someone who has been bereaved; whether we should approach them directly if we meet them by chance.

Would it not be best to leave them to it, or hope they will come to us when they are ready? Do we just ignore them, and leave them to it? Bereaved people so often tell me of the intense hurt and feeling of rejection, in addition to their pain, when those they know literally cross over to the other side of the road in order to avoid meeting them. The bereaved need their situation acknowledged by the outside world. They do not need abandoning in their prison of overwhelming grief.

So, acknowledge it. Go to them, for they are afraid of embarrassing you by inflicting their pain on you. A gentle touch on the arm, a reaching for their hand: 'I'm sorry to hear about your husband/wife/child/friend.' Just a gesture to show you care. There isn't a 'right' thing to say. Grief in itself may seem unbearable, but grief in isolation can be even worse. Just to know that someone cares and reaches out in love brings some measure of warmth and comfort which must never be underestimated. If you know them quite well, and it is some time since the death of their loved one, then ask them how they are – really – and be prepared to listen. You need not be afraid of opening wounds; the wounds are there, open, and may be tended by your listening and concern.

You may go from your church to visit someone you do not know, for whose relative your priest or minister has taken the funeral and has asked you to see how they are. It always helps if the priest mentions to the bereaved that he would like one of his parishioners to call round and see how they are. Most people are touched by the concern of the church and will welcome you. But if they do not want a visit then they have the opportunity to say so to the minister.

Do pause before you go, and pray that Christ may go with you. Of course he is with you. He never leaves you. But pray that you may be aware of his presence; that you will be what the bereaved person needs you to be; that you will bring a little light into their darkness. Then, knock on the door, gently but firmly, and stand well back so as not to appear intrusive. When the door opens you could say, 'Mrs White?' or, 'I've come to see Mrs

White,' if it is obviously not her; then state slowly and clearly who you are, and why you have come: 'I'm Jane Brown from All Saints. Our vicar took the funeral and he asked me to come and see how you are now.'

You will most likely be asked in. Most people are surprised and pleased that the church cares enough to send someone to see how they are. You will probably have the task of breaking the ice, for you are the one reaching out to them. It may help you to take some flowers or a plant – something in your hand to give – but it is not necessary. If there are flowers or cards around, you may like to comment on them. It could lead to a comment that 'Everyone has been so kind.' If there are photographs around you could ask if they are of family, and it could lead to an indication of whether family are nearby and supportive, or whether they have returned to living at a distance.

Do accept a cup of tea even if, like me, you prefer coffee. It gives your host an opportunity to give something to you, and sharing a cup of tea – or coffee – puts you on an equal basis. It is polite to ask where they would like you to sit. If you sit on 'his' chair you could start off on the wrong foot.

Don't be afraid of silences. The bereaved may be slow to get their thoughts together, and they will be feeling their way as to how much it is safe for them to say. So try to sit in a relaxed position, with an open and attentive attitude, ready to receive what they have to say. And let your attitude towards them be one of unconditional acceptance and love. It will be conveyed and is likely to open up channels of communication.

Mention the deceased by name if you can. The bereaved soon find out that many people are embarrassed to mention the name of their loved one, whereas what they often want to do more than anything else is to talk about them. So show them that this is all right with you; they will find great comfort in talking about the one who has died, and the tears may begin to flow. Let the tears come. There may be an attempt to check them, or to apologise, but tears are healing and relieving and a necessary part of grieving.

It is actually very painful to witness another's pain through crying and it may even bring tears to your eyes. That is all right. It is oddly comforting to have someone sharing to that extent in one's grief. Just stay quietly with them, or gently put your hand on theirs, or on their shoulder or arm. The power of touch can bring comfort and is an important part of sharing.

When it seems time to leave – and the first visit to someone you do not know is usually best to be quite short – get up from your seat and if it seems appropriate say, 'I'd like to come again, if that's all right with you.' The response is likely to be positive, but if they do not want another visit they will make excuses about not knowing when would be a good time, or having lots to do, and you will know. Do not take it as a personal rejection. If they do want you to come again, make a definite time, about a week or a fortnight ahead, and keep to that time. On the other hand, one visit may be enough, and you have shown that you, and the church, do care.

A visit, or sending flowers or a card, on the day of the anniversary of the death will almost always be appreciated, one year, two years, many years later. It comforts the bereaved to know that others remember and are willing to share with them a little in their loss.

After you leave, you may have a sense of overwhelming sadness, for you have shared in their sorrow. Stop for a short while before going on to anything else, and just offer the bereaved person and their situation to Christ; offer him your feelings, and the time you have spent with them; ask for his blessing on both of you, and then commit the whole visit to Jesus, and go on your way. If you really need to unload, then arrange a time with a trusted friend, preferably another bereavement visitor, and tell him or her how you feel, but never discuss what the bereaved has told you. You have been privileged to listen to some very personal facts and emotions, and what has been said must remain confidential. That is an essential part of pastoral visiting. It is between you, the bereaved, and Christ, and may safely be left there.

Father, I come before you now, a little unsure,
wanting only to reflect your compassion and bring
  your comfort.
Be with me as I visit the bereaved; bless both of us,
and use me as a channel of your grace. Amen.

19

THE MINISTRY OF LISTENING

It might bring confidence to some if I had provided a set of rules for responding to the bereaved. I hope I have shown that there are no rules in bereavement care, for each bereavement is unique, bringing different feelings of loss to each individual. And we can never assume that we know how anyone else feels, even if we have experienced a like bereavement.

The only rule which I can offer is this: listen, that you might find out what they are feeling and then try to be with them where they are.

A woman I was seeing in prison, who was working through her problems with a probation officer, a psychologist and a counsellor, wrote this about listening:

> You are *not* listening to me when:
>> You say you understand;
>> You have an answer for my problem before
>>> I've finished telling you my problem;
>> You cut me off before I've finished speaking;
>> You finish my sentences for me;

You are dying to tell me something;

You tell me about your experiences, making mine seem unimportant;

You refuse my thanks by saying you really haven't done anything.

You *are* listening when:

You really try to understand me, even if I'm not making much sense;

You grasp my point of view, even when it's against your own sincere convictions;

You realise that the hour I took from you has left you a bit tired and drained;

You allow me the dignity of making my own decisions, even though you think they might be wrong;

You do not take my problem from me, but allow me to deal with it in my own way;

You hold back the desire to give me good advice;

You do not offer me religious solace when you sense I am not ready for it;

You give me enough room to discover for myself what is really going on;

You accept my gratitude by telling me how good it makes you feel to know that you have been helpful.

How good a listener are you, really? We would all like to think we are good listeners, but just try this little exercise. Next time someone is telling you a story about what happened to them, check yourself to see how often you interrupt before they have paused in telling you their story. If you do wait until they pause or finish, do you immediately respond with a story of something similar that happened to you, and how you felt about it? This belittles their story, as you are talking about your own feelings which are quite irrelevant to them. Do you offer your opinion on what has happened to them, or a possible solution – your solution?

Most of us want to do all these things. Their experiences trigger off our own, and we want to tell them – or even cap theirs with something more dramatic, imagining that we are showing them that we understand. There may be a place for this at a dinner party, but it is not listening in a helpful way that will maintain their feelings of self-worth and make them feel understood and valued.

So what is good listening? I will call it a ministry for it is a total giving of ourselves to the other to help them feel understood, valued as a person, accepted as they are, and loved.

The first step in good listening is to make it clear

that you would like to hear what they have to say. I usually find that most bereaved people want to talk and need no more encouragement that your time and a friendly attitude. Try not to check their flow, other than an encouraging 'Yes', or, 'Do go on.' Hold back your own opinions or judgements and try to accept their pain, however unbearable it is. When they seem to have finished, leave a short silence to show that you are absorbing what they have said, and to give them the chance to add more if they want.

If they are only telling you the facts about what happened, try to explore their feelings. These may have been pushed down because the pain seems too much to bear but it is important for these to be faced if there is to be healing and rebuilding.

'How does all that make you feel?' you may ask. If the reply is 'I don't know', you may like to hazard a guess at their feelings: 'That must make you feel so hurt.' If you have got it right they will feel understood and go on. If you have got it wrong they will want to correct you: 'No, I don't feel hurt, I feel angry.' That is all right. It is not a rebuff. You have shown that you are trying to understand and they will appreciate that. Occasionally they may say, 'I don't want to talk about it' – and that has to be all right.

They may say things that make you feel

uncomfortable: 'I just hate that doctor for not giving him more pain relievers' or, 'I don't want to be invited out. I feel jealous of all married couples.' It is good for people to express their very real negative feelings; they begin to lose their power when they are released. Rather than contradict this kind of statement you may like to say, with sincerity, 'I think I can understand why you feel that.' As long as you show that you accept them, however they feel, they will usually be greatly helped by getting out their worst feelings.

It will even help them if they feel they can say to you, 'I just feel I don't want to go on living.' It is often said, for that is how many of the bereaved feel, but just check it out. Ask if they have ever thought seriously about ending it all. They will usually look quite shocked and reply that they would never do anything like that; it is just that they do not see much point to life at the moment. If they hesitate, however, ask if they have thought how they would do it, and if they come out with a well-thought-out plan of suicide, then you must pass this information on to a relative, or try to get them to see a doctor, or to see or phone the Samaritans. You cannot be burdened with this knowledge without taking some action.

The real difficulty of listening to the bereaved is that we want to say something that will make them feel better; to suggest how they might tackle things; to tell them they will get over it. It is hard for us to accept and bear their feelings of pain. Yet it seems to me that in quietly sharing and bearing we can somehow take upon ourselves a little of their pain for a while.

Remember again the needs of those who are bereaved: they need to overcome their intense feelings of isolation by finding those who are prepared to listen and hear how they are feeling; they need to feel normal, that they are not going mad, that their overwhelming feelings are only to be expected considering the loss they are experiencing; they need to express their feelings and still feel accepted, loved and supported as the people they are.

Remember that at the point when they feel understood they will experience relief. And as they feel loved they will have the energy to rebuild their lives and to try to find meaning in it without the one they have loved and lost.

Listening is a ministry which is well worth practising for it is both healing and restoring. Try to have confidence in its value for it is the kind of confidence you may know in helping the bereaved. You have been given the gift of compassion for those who suffer, and in taking up the ministry of listening you will bring to them that of

God in you which will touch that of God in them, whether or not they are aware of it.

Father of all, as I try to listen to those who are
    suffering bereavement,
give me the grace to hear with your love, to try to
    understand,
to accept them completely, for your sake.
So give me the confidence to reach out to the
    bereaved,
and to offer them all that I am, in the name of
    Jesus Christ. Amen.

20
REVIEW

And now let us return to that Swiss mountainside with its little white church and brilliantly flowered graves. May I ask if you feel any more confident now that you can offer something of value to those people who planted the flowers?

I hope so. I hope that you might be more aware of the Christ-light of love within you responding to the 'light that enlightens everyone' within them, whether or not they know Christ for themselves.

As we look again we shall see that some graves have a small photograph of the one who has died – a remembrance of the individual with all his or her joys and pain, achievements and failures, relationships and love. You know how the bereaved will want to talk about these things and express their feelings of loss, as they face their own lives now without that loved one. And you are practising the ministry of listening, that you may hear them with quiet, unjudgemental acceptance and a warm, loving attitude.

Underneath the photograph is the small crucifix, the remembrance that Christ died for that person whose body lies in the grave, that they might have eternal ife. To us it is a remembrance that Christ died for us too, for you and for me, that we might know eternal life here and now through faith and love in him as our living Lord.

Our eyes may wander over the flowers to the enclosed red candle which is always burning. A symbol of the light of Christ which never goes out; a reminder of the much brighter light seen only in heaven.

The cross of Christ is still a mystery to most of us. Death is still an unknown experience, and eternal life may only be glimpsed by our earth-bound minds. But over and above our human understanding there is faith, that gift from God which transcends our limited minds and lifts us to another realm where worship takes the place of relating; where the receiving of God's love fills all the emptiness of our human hearts. Nourishing our faith, albeit the tiny grain of faith which is in all who seek, is our preparation for reaching out to the bereaved. It is the firm base from which you will go out, with reassurance and inner peace.

As faith in God is the key to our preparation, so love for the one we are going to see is the key to our communication with them. This is the love that accepts the whole person, that gives without expecting anything in return, the love that perseveres.

The secret of this is in the giving. As you start by giving whatever love you can – and remember it is that love that made you want to help the bereaved – it will increase as you show you care about them and listen to how they feel. And when they feel you are with them where they are, in understanding and acceptance, that love will burst into something greater than yours. You are offering the very love of Christ – and you may safely leave the rest in his hands.

For it is Jesus who wants to help the bereaved, and he is gracious enough to use me, and you, as part of his body on earth.

Let us now draw our life from him and go out in his name to take up our share of his redeeming work on earth as we respond to those who have been bereaved.

May I close with a prayer for you, my readers, that you may be truly blessed in this work:

> May the kingdom of God be established in your
> hearts and lives;
> and may you bring his love to all you meet, in
> Jesus' name.

Now to him who is able to do immeasurably more
    than all we ask or imagine,
according to his power that is at work within us,
to him be glory in the church and in Christ Jesus
    throughout all generations, for ever and ever!
Amen (Ephesians 3.20–1).